CAMBRIDGE PRIMARY
Science

Skills Builder

Jon Board and Alan Cross

CAMBRIDGE
UNIVERSITY PRESS

University Printing House, Cambridge CB2 8BS, United Kingdom

One Liberty Plaza, 20th Floor, New York, NY 10006, USA

477 Williamstown Road, Port Melbourne, VIC 3207, Australia

314–321, 3rd Floor, Plot 3, Splendor Forum, Jasola District Centre, New Delhi – 110025, India

79 Anson Road, #06–04/06, Singapore 079906

Cambridge University Press is part of the University of Cambridge.

It furthers the University's mission by disseminating knowledge in the pursuit of education, learning and research at the highest international levels of excellence.

Information on this title: education.cambridge.org

© Cambridge University Press 2016

This publication is in copyright. Subject to statutory exception and to the provisions of relevant collective licensing agreements, no reproduction of any part may take place without the written permission of Cambridge University Press.

First published 2016

20 19 18 17 16 15 14 13

Produced for Cambridge University Press by White-Thomson Publishing
www.wtpub.co.uk

Editor: Rachel Minay
Designer: Tracey Camden

Printed in Malaysia by Vivar Printing

A catalogue record for this publication is available from the British Library

ISBN 978-1-316-61101-2 Paperback

Cambridge University Press has no responsibility for the persistence or accuracy of URLs for external or third-party internet websites referred to in this publication, and does not guarantee that any content on such websites is, or will remain, accurate or appropriate. Information regarding prices, travel timetables, and other factual information given in this work is correct at the time of first printing but Cambridge University Press does not guarantee the accuracy of such information thereafter.

Cover artwork: Bill Bolton

NOTICE TO TEACHERS IN THE UK

It is illegal to reproduce any part of this work in material form (including photocopying and electronic storage) except under the following circumstances:
(i) where you are abiding by a licence granted to your school or institution by the Copyright Licensing Agency;
(ii) where no such licence exists, or where you wish to exceed the terms of a licence, and you have gained the written permission of Cambridge University Press;
(iii) where you are allowed to reproduce without permission under the provisions of Chapter 3 of the Copyright, Designs and Patents Act 1988, which covers, for example, the reproduction of short passages within certain types of educational anthology and reproduction for the purposes of setting examination questions.

Contents

Introduction	4
1 Going outside	5
1.1 Different places to live	6
1.2 Can we care for our environment?	8
1.3 Our weather	10
2 Looking at rocks	11
2.1 What are rocks?	12
2.2 Uses of rocks	13
2.3 Soil	15
2.4 Other natural materials	16
3 Changing materials	17
3.2 Bending and twisting	18
3.3 Fantastic elastic	19
3.4 Heating and cooling	21
3.5 Why is the sea salty?	23
4 Light and dark	25
4.1 Different light sources	26
4.2 Darkness	27
4.4 Shadow shapes	28
5 Electricity	30
5.1 Electricity around us	31
5.2 Staying safe	33
5.3 Making a circuit	34
5.5 Switches	35
6 The Earth and the Sun	37
6.1 Day and night	38
6.2 Does the Sun move?	40
6.3 Changing shadows	42
Answers	43
Glossary	48

Introduction

This series of primary science activity books complements *Cambridge Primary Science* and promotes, through practice, learner confidence and depth of knowledge in the skills of scientific enquiry (SE) and key scientific vocabulary and concepts. These activity books will:

- enhance and extend learners' scientific knowledge and facts
- promote scientific enquiry skills and learning in order to think like a scientist
- advance each learner's knowledge and use of scientific vocabulary and concepts in their correct context.

The *Skills Builder* activity books consolidate core topics that learners have *already* covered in the classroom, providing those learners with that extra reinforcement of SE skills, vocabulary topic knowledge and understanding. They have been written with a focus on scientific literacy with ESL/EAL learners in mind.

How to use the activity books

These activity books have been designed for use by individual learners, either in the classroom or at home. As teachers and as parents, you can decide how and when they are used by your learner to best improve their progress. The *Skills Builder* activity books target specific topics (lessons) from Grades 1–6 from all the units covered in *Cambridge Primary Science*. This targeted approach has been carefully designed to consolidate topics where help is most needed.

How to use the units

Unit introduction

Each unit starts with an introduction for you as the teacher or parent. It clearly sets out which topics are covered in the unit and the learning objectives of the activities in each section. This is where you can work with learners to select all, most or just one of the sections according to individual needs.

The introduction also provides advice and tips on how best to support the learner in the skills of scientific enquiry and in the practice of key scientific vocabulary.

At this grade, it is very likely the learners are still learning to read, so teacher/parent may need to explain these verbally.

Sections

Each section matches a corresponding lesson in the main series. Sections contain write-in activities that are supported by:

- Key words – key vocabulary for the topic, also highlighted in bold in the sections
- Key facts – a short fact to support the activities where relevant
- Look and learn – where needed, activities are supported with scientific exemplars for extra support of how to treat a concept or scientific method
- Remember – tips for the learner to steer them in the right direction.

How to approach the write-in activities

Teachers and parents are advised to provide students with a blank A5 notebook at the start of each grade for learners to use alongside these activity books. Most activities will provide enough space for the answers required. However, some learner responses – especially to enquiry-type questions – may require more space for notes. Keeping notes and plans models how scientists work and encourages learners to explore and record their thinking, leaving the activity books for the final, more focused answers.

Think about it questions

Each unit also contains some questions for discussion at home with parents, or at school. Although learners will record the outcomes of their discussions in the activity book, these questions are intended to encourage the students to think more deeply.

Self-assessment

Each section in the unit ends with a self-assessment opportunity for learners: empty circles with short learning statements. Teachers or parents can ask learners to complete the circles in a number of ways, depending on their age and preference, e.g. with faces, traffic light colours or numbers. The completed self-assessments provide teachers with a clearer understanding of how best to progress and support individual learners.

Glossary of key words and concepts

At the end of each activity book there is a glossary of key scientific words and concepts arranged by unit. Learners are regularly reminded to practise saying these words out loud and in sentences to improve communication skills in scientific literacy.

1 Going outside

What learners will practise and reinforce

The activities in this Skills Builder unit give learners further practice in the following topics in the Learner's Book and Activity Book:

Topic	In this topic, learners will:
1.1 Different places to live	collect evidence and present it in a Venn diagram
1.2 Can we care for our environment?	consider why we should look after the environment
1.3 Our weather	practise using weather vocabulary
1.4 Extreme weather	see Challenge, Section 1.4

Help your learner

In this unit, learners will practise making comparisons (Sections 1.1, 1.2 and 1.3), identifying patterns (Section 1.1), using simple information sources (Sections 1.1 and 1.3) and making and recording observations (Sections 1.1 and 1.3). To help them:

1 In Section 1.2, encourage learners to use first-hand experience to talk about environments they have visited that were not well looked after. Ask them to say how the damage to the environment made them feel.

2 In Section 1.3, learners could make regular observations of the weather. They could make weather cards to display on a poster to show what the weather is doing each day.

> ⚠ Help learners to practise using the animal names in Section 1.1 and the weather words in Section 1.3. Learners who find these easy to learn could be challenged to learn more weather words and animal names.

1.1 Different places to live

different, environment, Venn diagram

Sorting animals

1 Look at the animals in these two **different environments**.

2 Draw the animals in the right place in the **Venn diagram**.

Remember:

Animals that live in both environments go in the middle of the Venn diagram.

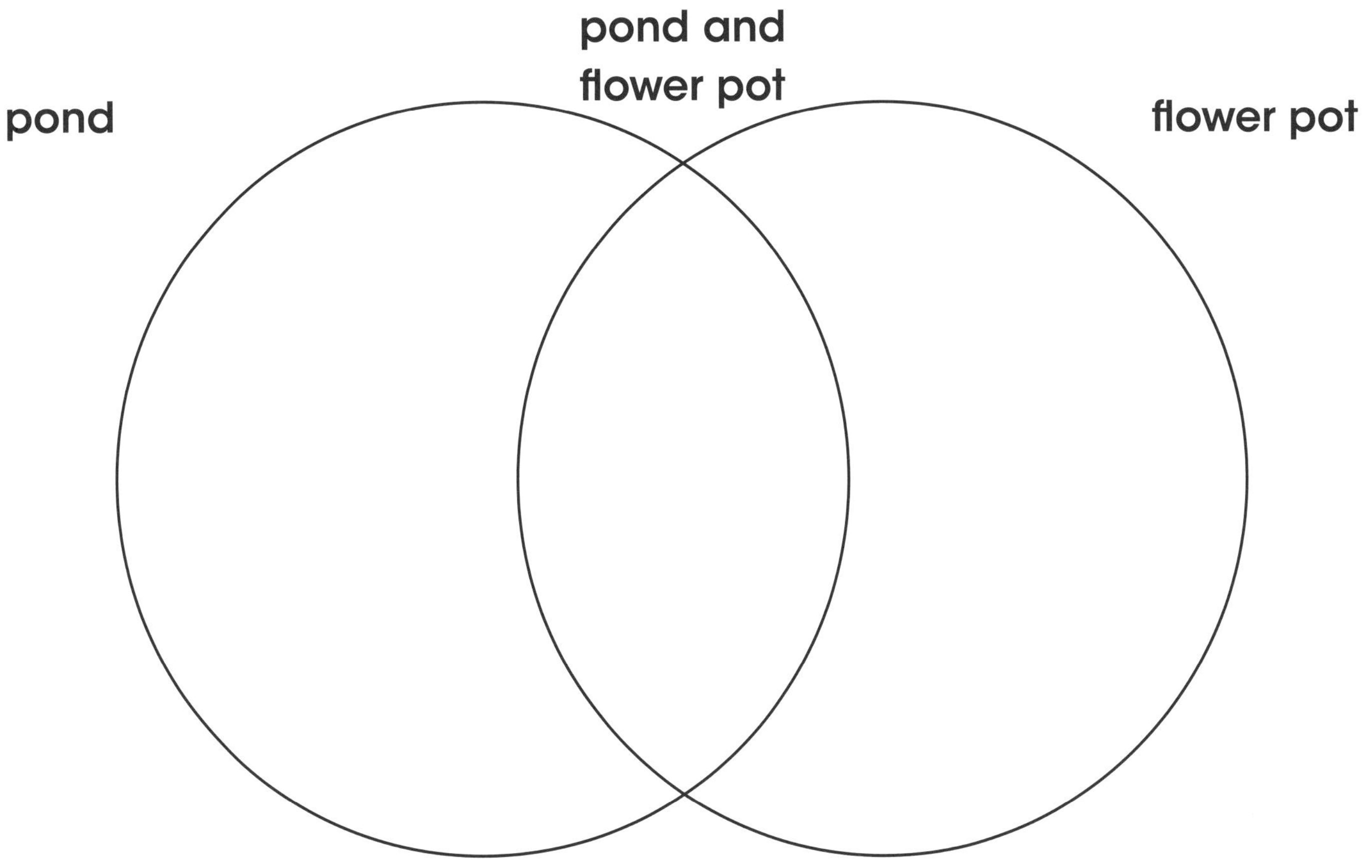

pond   pond and flower pot   flower pot

3 Use the key below to help you label each animal.

| snail | spider | worm | tadpole | fish |

4 Think about it!

Why can't a fish live in a flower pot?

_____

_____

CHECK YOUR LEARNING

○ I can compare different environments.

○ I can use a Venn diagram to sort things.

1 Going outside   7

1.2 Can we care for our environment?

litter

A better environment

Sometimes people do not look after the environment.

1 Cross out the **litter** and the damage to this environment.

2 Think about it!

Why is litter bad for animals?

_____

Now look at the environment. People are looking after it.

3 Colour in the picture.

CHECK YOUR LEARNING

◯ I know different ways to look after the environment.

1 Going outside

1.3 Our weather

temperature, hot, warm, cold, sunny, rainy, cloudy, snowy, windy, stormy

What is the weather like today?

1 Look at the table below. What is the weather in each picture?

2 What is the **temperature**? Hot, warm or **cold**?

LOOK AND LEARN

 sunny	 rainy
 cloudy	 snowy
 windy	 stormy

	Weather	Temperature
	snowy	cold

CHECK YOUR LEARNING

○ I can say what the weather is like.

2 Looking at rocks

What learners will practise and reinforce

The activities in this Skills Builder unit give learners further practice in the following topics in the Learner's Book and Activity Book:

Topic	In this topic, learners will:
2.1 What are rocks?	observe rocks and sort them into groups
2.2 Uses of rocks	test the hardness of rocks and decide which is best for making steps
2.3 Soil	observe small differences in a soil sample
2.4 Other natural materials	learn about natural and man-made materials

Help your learner

In this unit, learners will practise making observations to answer a science question (Sections 2.1, 2.2 and 2.3), making comparisons (Sections 2.1, 2.2 and 2.4) and keeping a test fair (Section 2.2). To help them:

1 To help learners understand the need for a fair test in Section 2.2, talk with them about how the test could be unfair for the rocks. Pretend to scratch one rock with great force and another very lightly. Ask learners to say what you are doing wrong.

2 For Section 2.3, learners could collect their own soil from a garden. Most learners will enjoy digging a small hole to see what they can find. Talk with them about what they expect to see before they start to dig.

TEACHING TIP

Encourage learners to start a collection of rocks they find themselves. Ask them which their favourite is. Some learners will enjoy turning their favourite rock into a 'pet rock' by gluing on eyes or other features drawn on paper.

2.1 What are rocks?

Sorting rocks

1 Collect 8–10 small rocks from outside. Wash and dry them.

2 Look carefully at the colour and shape of the rocks.

3 Put the rocks into groups that look the same. Give each group a name.

4 Draw your rock groups in this box.

CHECK YOUR LEARNING

◯ I can observe rocks carefully.

◯ I can sort rocks into groups.

2.2 Uses of rocks

hardest, fair, force, scratch

Which rock is hardest?

You will need three different rocks and a coin.

Kai is testing rocks to find out which is the **hardest**.

1 You are going to do the same test. What will you do to make the test **fair**?

Use the same **force** for each rock. ☐

Use a different force for each rock. ☐

Use the same coin for each rock. ☐

Use a different coin for each rock. ☐

2 Test your rocks and fill in the table. Use some of these words:

no scratch   very small scratch   small scratch
large scratch   very large scratch

	Rock 1	Rock 2	Rock 3
Is there a **scratch** on the rock?			

2 Looking at rocks 13

Think about it!

Steps need to be made from hard stone.

3 Which of your rocks would be the best for steps?

_____

_____

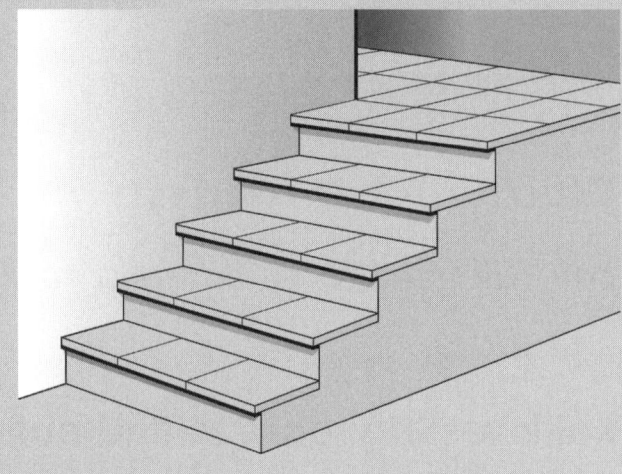

4 Why? _____

_____

CHECK YOUR LEARNING

◯ I can use a fair test to compare rocks.

2.3 Soil

soil, living, died, air

What is soil?

*You will need some **soil**, a magnifying glass and white paper.*

1 Put the soil on the paper.

2 What can you find? Draw some of the things you find here.

Living things	Things that have died	Small rocks

3 Think about it!

Some animals live in soil. Do you think there is **air** in soil?

yes ☐   no ☐

⚠️ Wash your hands after touching soil.

CHECK YOUR LEARNING

○ I can look carefully to see small differences in soil.

2.4 Other natural materials

natural, man-made, cotton, wood, milk

Where do natural materials come from?

1 Match these **natural** materials with where they come from.

LOOK AND LEARN

Natural materials come from nature. They are not made by people.

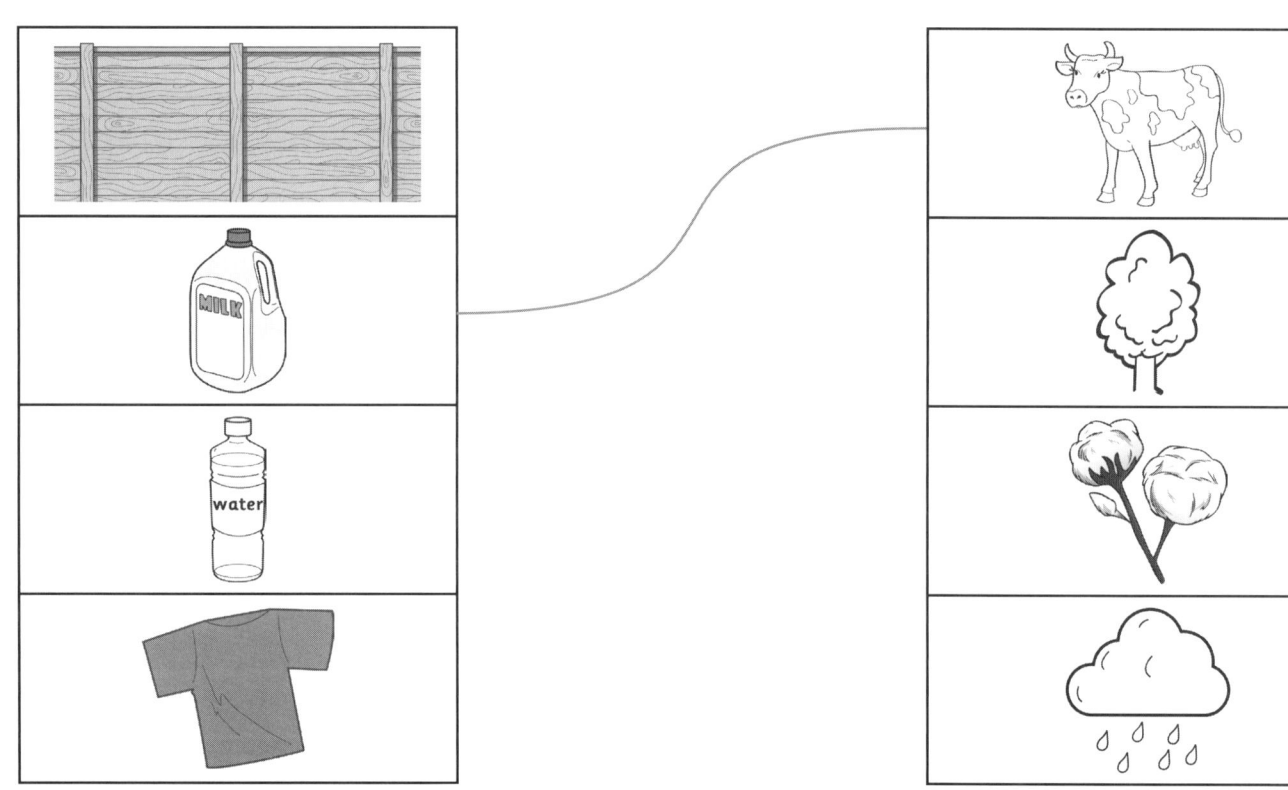

2 Think about it!

Paper is not a natural material. People make paper from wood.

Write three other **man-made** materials here.

_____   _____   _____

CHECK YOUR LEARNING

◯   I know that some materials are natural and some are man-made.

3 Changing materials

What learners will practise and reinforce

The activities in this Skills Builder unit give learners further practice in the following topics in the Learner's Book and Activity Book:

Topic	In this topic, learners will:
3.1 Materials changing shape	see Challenge, Section 3.1
3.2 Bending and twisting	investigate materials that bend or twist
3.3 Fantastic elastic	sort materials by whether they are elastic or not
3.4 Heating and cooling	observe that solids melt to form liquids
3.5 Why is the sea salty?	explain what happened in an investigation

Help your learner

In this unit, learners will practise making and recording observations (Section 3.2). They will also practise making predictions (Section 3.3) and comparisons (Section 3.4), and explaining what happened (Section 3.5). To help them:

1 Make up an action for the key words 'bend', 'twist', 'stretch' and 'squash'. Learners could then play a game such as 'Simon Says' to practise using the words and the actions.

2 Help learners to investigate other melting solids. Help them to safely melt butter or chocolate in a saucepan or in a microwave.

⚠ Help learners to stay safe near cooking equipment.

TEACHING TIP

There are many opportunities to watch materials change when heated or cooled in the kitchen. If possible, help learners to do some simple cooking. Talk with them about the changes they see.

3.2 Bending and twisting

bend, twist

Materials that bend and twist

You will need a sheet of paper, a metal paper clip, a cotton T-shirt, a metal coin and a plastic ruler.

1 Try to **bend** and **twist** each object.

2 Fill in the table. One has been started for you.

Object	Material	Bend	Twist
sheet of paper	paper	✓	✓

KEY FACT

Look at your results. Most materials that can bend can also twist.

3 **Think about it!**

In what way would clothes made from metal change the way you move?

_____

_____

CHECK YOUR LEARNING

◯ I can record my observations in a table.

◯ I know that some materials can bend or twist.

3.3 Fantastic elastic

elastic, stretch, squash

Testing elastic materials

You will need a sponge, a sheet of paper, a rubber band, a paper clip and three other objects.

LOOK AND LEARN

Elastic materials go back into shape after being bent, **stretched**, **squashed** or twisted.

1 Do you think these materials are elastic?

sponge	paper	rubber band	paper clip
elastic ☐	elastic ☐	elastic ☐	elastic ☐
not elastic ☐	not elastic ☐	not elastic ☐	not elastic ☐

2 Try to bend, stretch, squash or twist the objects. If they go back into shape, they are elastic. Were you right?

_____
_____
_____
_____

KEY FACT

Rubber is an elastic material. It makes this rubber ball bounce.

3 Changing materials   **19**

3 Now find and test three other objects.

4 Draw each object in the table. Write the material each is made from.

Elastic	Not elastic
rubber	

5 Think about it!
Name some toys that use elastic materials.

CHECK YOUR LEARNING

◯ I can test materials to find out if they are elastic.

3.4 Heating and cooling

heat, solid, melt, liquid, ice

LOOK AND LEARN

We can use **heat** to make a **solid** material **melt** into a **liquid**.

This chocolate is melting in the Sun.

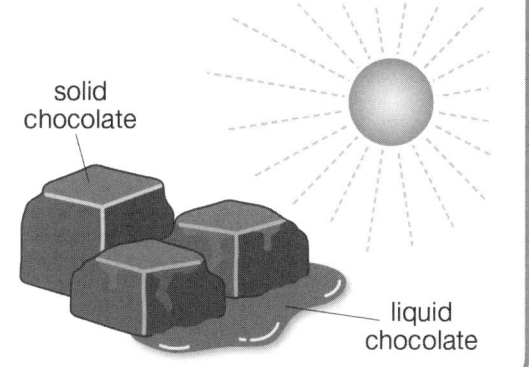

solid chocolate

liquid chocolate

A melting candle

This wax candle is melting when it gets close to the flame.

1 Label the wax that is solid.

2 Label the wax that is liquid.

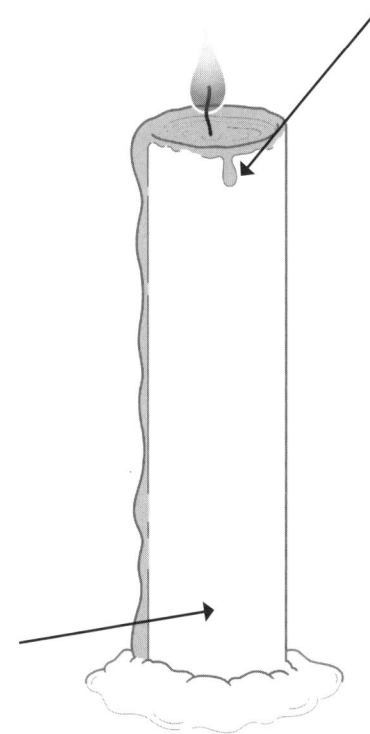

3 Changing materials

Melting ice

You will need an *ice* cube and a fridge or freezer.

1 Take an ice cube and watch it melt.

2 Draw the ice cube as it melts and afterwards. Label the solid and liquid parts.

3 How can you make the water turn back into solid ice?

make it colder ☐   heat it ☐

4 **Think about it!**

What has happened to the rock inside this volcano?

_____

_____

CHECK YOUR LEARNING

◯ I can say what happens to a solid when it is heated.

3.4 Heating and cooling

3.5 Why is the sea salty?

`dissolve`

LOOK AND LEARN

Some materials **dissolve**.

Some do not.

Dissolved or not?

Tia has been trying to dissolve different materials in water.

1 Write what has happened for each material.

    The flour has not dissolved.

    _____

3 Changing materials   23

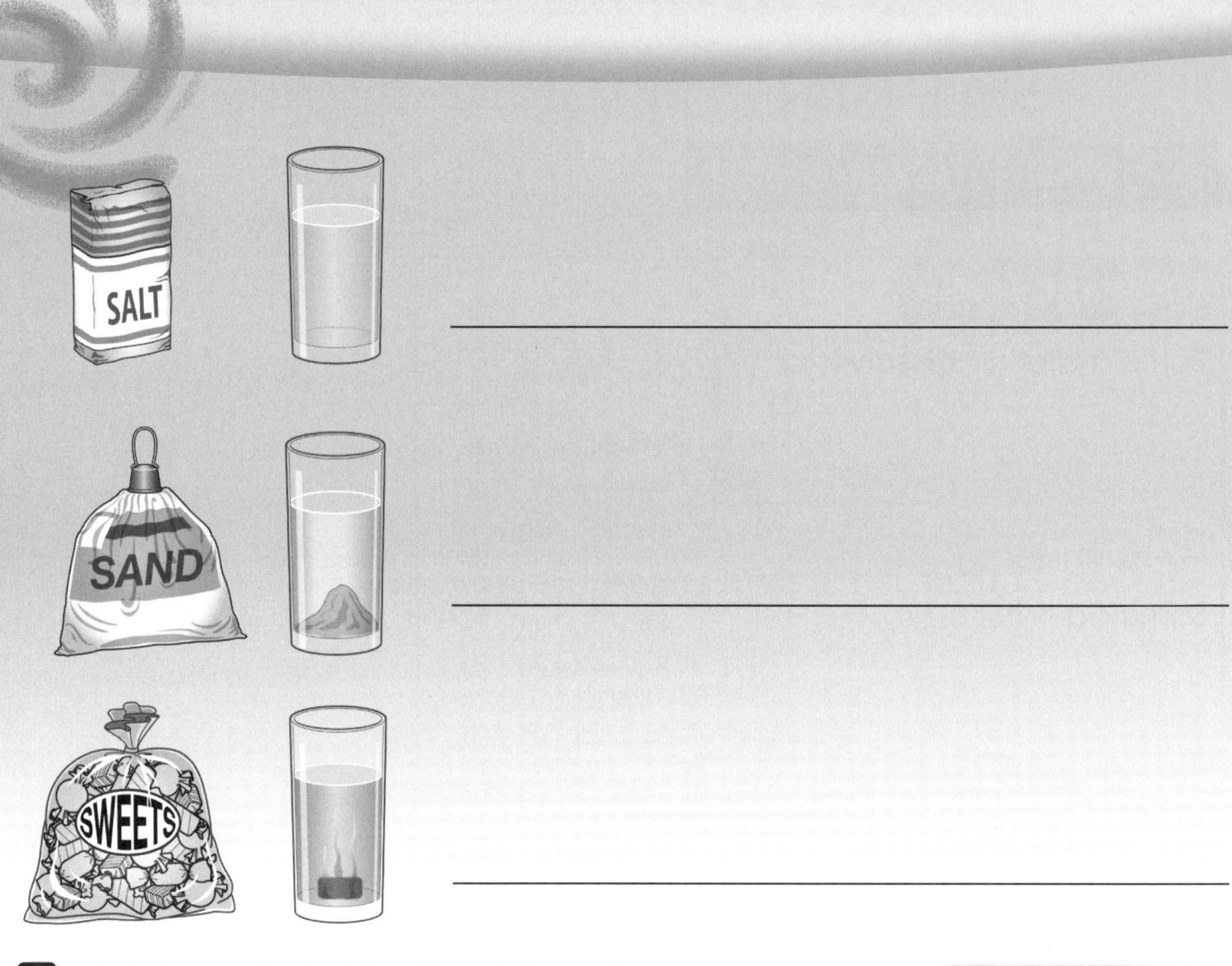

2 Which material is dissolving slowly in the pictures?

_____

CHECK YOUR LEARNING

○ I can make observations and explain what happened.

○ I know that some materials dissolve in water.

KEY FACT

Some materials dissolve slowly. Some dissolve quickly.

3.5 Why is the sea salty?

4 Light and dark

What learners will practise and reinforce

The activities in this Skills Builder unit give learners further practice in the following topics in the Learner's Book and Activity Book:

Topic	In this topic, learners will:
4.1 Light sources	recognise that there are many light sources, for example the Sun, and that they all make light
4.2 Darkness	understand that darkness is a lack of light and that without light we cannot see
4.3 Making shadows	see Challenge, Section 4.3
4.4 Shadow shapes	see that shadows look dark and can have a shape that is different to the object that makes them

Help your learner

In this unit, learners will collect evidence by making observations when trying to answer a science question (Section 4.4) and use first-hand experience (Sections 4.2 and 4.4). To help them:

1 In Section 4.2, help learners to set up the 'Can I see in the tent?' activity. It is best if you can use quite opaque fabric and do this in a darkened room.

TEACHING TIP

Light is very familiar to us as we experience it every day. It is important to use the science terms correctly. For example be very clear that the Sun is a light source, but the Moon is not.

4.1 Light sources

light, Sun, Moon, reflect

Different light sources

Look at the picture and draw a circle around each light source.

LOOK AND LEARN

A light source is something that makes **light**, for example the **Sun**.

CHECK YOUR LEARNING

◯ I know that there are many light sources, including the Sun.

◯ I know that light sources make their own light.

KEY FACT

The **Moon** is not a light source. The Moon **reflects** light from the Sun.

26 4.1 Light sources

4.2 Darkness

> torch, dark

Can I see in the tent?

*You will need sheets or blankets, a **torch** and white, black and shiny objects.*

"It looks dark in there."

1. Make a tent that is **dark** inside. Put some objects in the tent.

2. Which objects are easier to see in the dark?

   _____

   _____

3. Which objects are harder to see?

   _____

4. Use the torch. Are the objects easier to see? _____

5. **Think about it!**

   Is your bedroom completely dark at night? If you can see at all, then there must be some light. Where does the light come from?

   _____

CHECK YOUR LEARNING

◯ I know that we cannot see without some light.

4.4 Shadow shapes

shadow

Shadow show!

Look at the shadow shapes. What can you see?

1. _____a girl_____
2. _____
3. _____
4. _____
5. _____
6. _____
7. _____
8. _____

Turn it, change it

You will need a torch and some different objects.

The same object can make different shadows.

1. Shine the torch onto an object to make its shadow.
2. Draw the shape of the shadow.
3. Now turn the object. Draw the new shape of the shadow.
4. Do the same for your other objects.

Object	Shadow	Shadow after turning
👞	👞	👞

CHECK YOUR LEARNING

○ I know that shadows can look very different from the objects that make them.

5 Electricity

What learners will practise and reinforce

The activities in this Skills Builder unit give learners further practice in the following topics in the Learner's Book and Activity Book:

Topic	In this topic, learners will:
5.1 Electricity around us	see that electricity is very useful learn that electricity comes from the mains or from cells
5.2 Staying safe	know how to keep safe around mains electricity
5.3 Making a circuit	recognise a working circuit know that a bulb uses electricity to make light
5.4 Using motors and buzzers	see Challenge, Section 5.4
5.5 Switches	see how switches can turn electricity on and off

Help your learner

In this unit, learners will practise using first-hand experience (Sections 5.1, 5.3 and 5.5), predict what will happen before deciding what to do (Section 5.5), talk about risks and how to avoid danger (Section 5.2) and review and explain what happened (Section 5.3).

TEACHING TIP

Note to teachers/parents: Safety when using electricity and identifying whether objects use mains electricity or cells are both additional to the framework at this grade stage.

⚠ Learners should only ever handle low voltage cells and batteries (1.5v – 9v). They should learn about the serious danger of mains electricity and to avoid contact with mains plugs, sockets and switches, and any damaged mains wires or components. They should also learn about the danger of liquids and electricity.

5.1 Electricity around us

electricity, mains electricity, cell, battery

LOOK AND LEARN

Electricity is very useful. It makes lots of things work.

Things that we plug in use **mains electricity**.

Small electrical things often use **cells**. (A cell is often called a **battery**.)

mains electricity

electricity from cells

Does it use electricity?

1 Colour in the objects that use electricity.

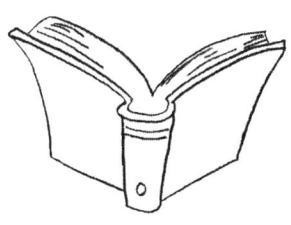

2 Which of these objects use mains electricity and which use a cell? Tick one box.

	mains electricity	cell		mains electricity	cell
TV remote	☐	☐	lamp	☐	☐
calculator	☐	☐	washing machine	☐	☐

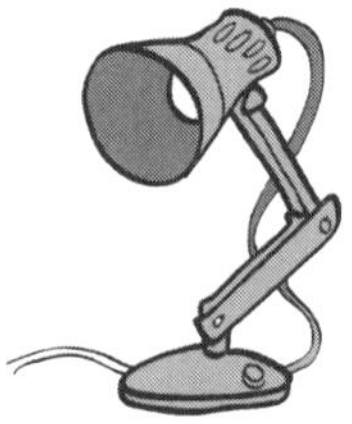

Electricity around me

You will need a notepad and pen, or a camera.

1 Walk around your home or school and photograph or note the things that use electricity.

2 Say if they use mains electricity or cells.

⚠️ Do not handle plugs and mains electricity; it is very dangerous.

3 **Think about it!**

There are people in some places who still live without electricity. What would you miss the most if you lived without electricity?

_____

CHECK YOUR LEARNING

◯ I know that electricity is very useful.

◯ I know that electricity comes from mains electricity or from cells.

5.1 Electricity around us

5.2 Staying safe

electric shock, wire, power cables

Danger, danger!

Look at the picture.

> **Remember:**
>
> Mains electricity can give you a dangerous **electric shock**!
>
> Keep safe by:
> - keeping water away from electricity
> - never using damaged **wire**
> - never putting things other than a plug in a wall socket.

1 Circle each of the dangerous things you can see in the picture.

2 Talk to your friends about these dangers and ways to stay safe.

CHECK YOUR LEARNING

◯ I know that mains electricity is very dangerous.

◯ I know how to keep safe around mains wires and sockets.

KEY FACT

You will see **power cables** across your streets and homes. Children are killed every year playing too close to these. Never climb or play near them.

5 Electricity 33

5.3 Making a circuit

bulb, circuit, connected, working circuit

My electric circuit

*You will need a cell, wire and a **bulb**.*

1 Look at the **circuit** around this page. Can you see the cell, the wire, the bulb?

There are no gaps. All the parts are **connected** and the bulb is lit. The bulb uses electricity to make light.

Use your finger to follow the arrows around the circuit. This is how the electricity moves.

2 Use the wire, cell and bulb to make your own circuit.

3 Did your circuit work? If so, explain why.

_____

_____

CHECK YOUR LEARNING

○ I can recognise a **working circuit**.

○ I know that a bulb uses electricity to make light.

Remember: A circuit will only work if the metal parts of the wire, cell and bulb are connected.

34   5.3 Making a circuit

5.5 Switches

switch, predict

Make a switch with a straw!

You will need a cell, a bulb, wire, a plastic straw, a metal paper clip and a rubber band or sticky tape.

LOOK AND LEARN

We can turn electricity on or off using a **switch**.

This circuit has a gap. The bulb will not light up.

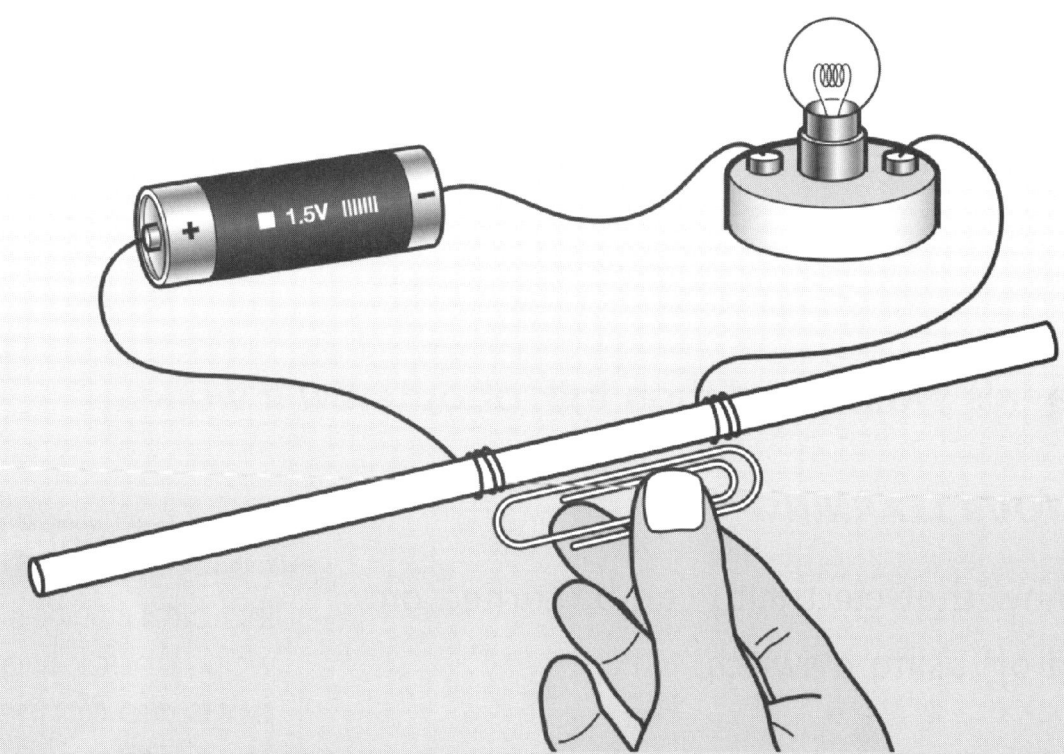

1 **Predict** what will happen if the metal clip touches both wires.

_____

_____

2 Now make this circuit and test the metal clip. Make sure all the metal parts are touching.

5 Electricity 35

3 Look at the picture to see how to make a switch. By moving the metal clip, you can turn the switch on or off.

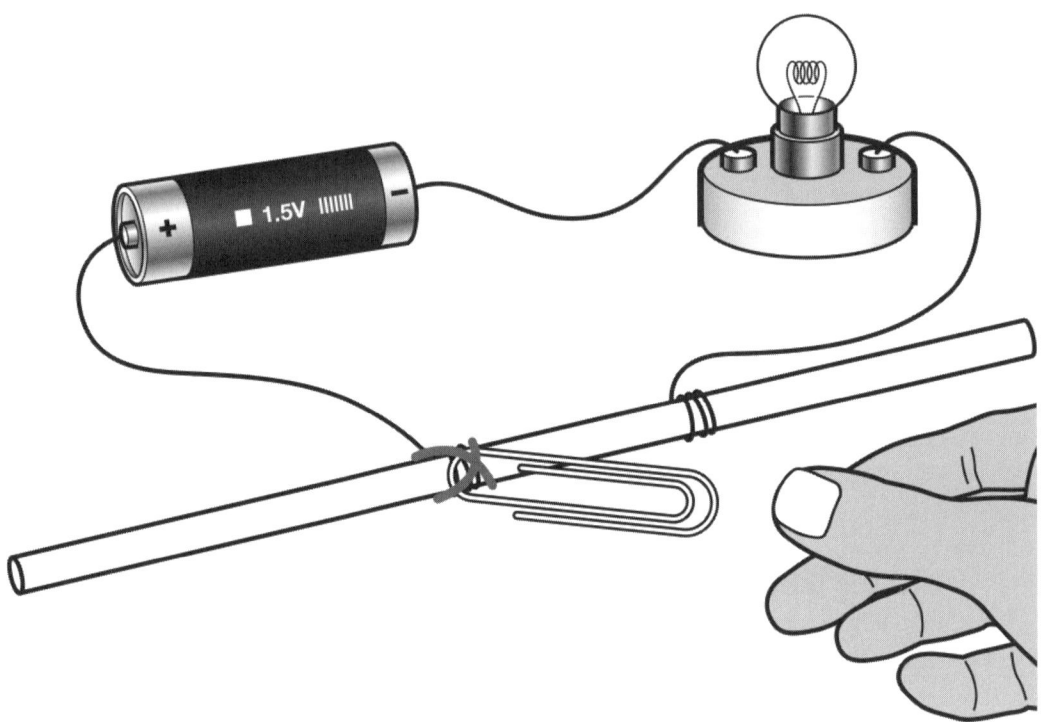

4 Make this switch and then talk about how it works.

CHECK YOUR LEARNING

○ I know that electricity can be turned on and off using a switch.

Remember:
If a circuit does not work, check that all parts are connected. Try a different bulb and cell.

6 The Earth and the Sun

What learners will practise and reinforce

The activities in this Skills Builder unit give learners further practice in the following topics in the Learner's Book and Activity Book:

Topic	In this topic, learners will:
6.1 Day and night	explore how we get day and night because the Earth spins
6.2 Does the Sun move?	understand that it looks like the Sun is moving because the Earth spins
6.3 Changing shadows	see that shadows move solely as the Earth spins and observe that shadows are short when the Sun is high and long when the Sun is low

Help your learner

In this unit, learners will practise making predictions (Sections 6.1–6.3) and collecting evidence by making observations when trying to answer a science question (Sections 6.2 and 6.3). They will also use a variety of ways to tell others what happened (Section 6.2) and recognise that a test or comparison may be unfair (Section 6.3). To help them:

> ⚠ Remind learners they should never look straight at the Sun.

1 Encourage learners to select and assemble equipment themselves. Ask them to explain why they need each piece of equipment.

TEACHING TIP

Help learners to see that they live on a spinning planet, which means that very distant things in the sky appear to move when this effect is really caused by the spinning of the Earth. Learners may find this challenging and slip back to incorrect ideas.

6.1 Day and night

spin, day, night

City in the day or night?

Look at this picture of the Earth. Can you see the cities Delhi and Jakarta?

LOOK AND LEARN

The Earth is like a **spinning** ball. Light from the Sun means that when one side of the Earth is in the light, the other side is dark. This makes **day** and **night**.

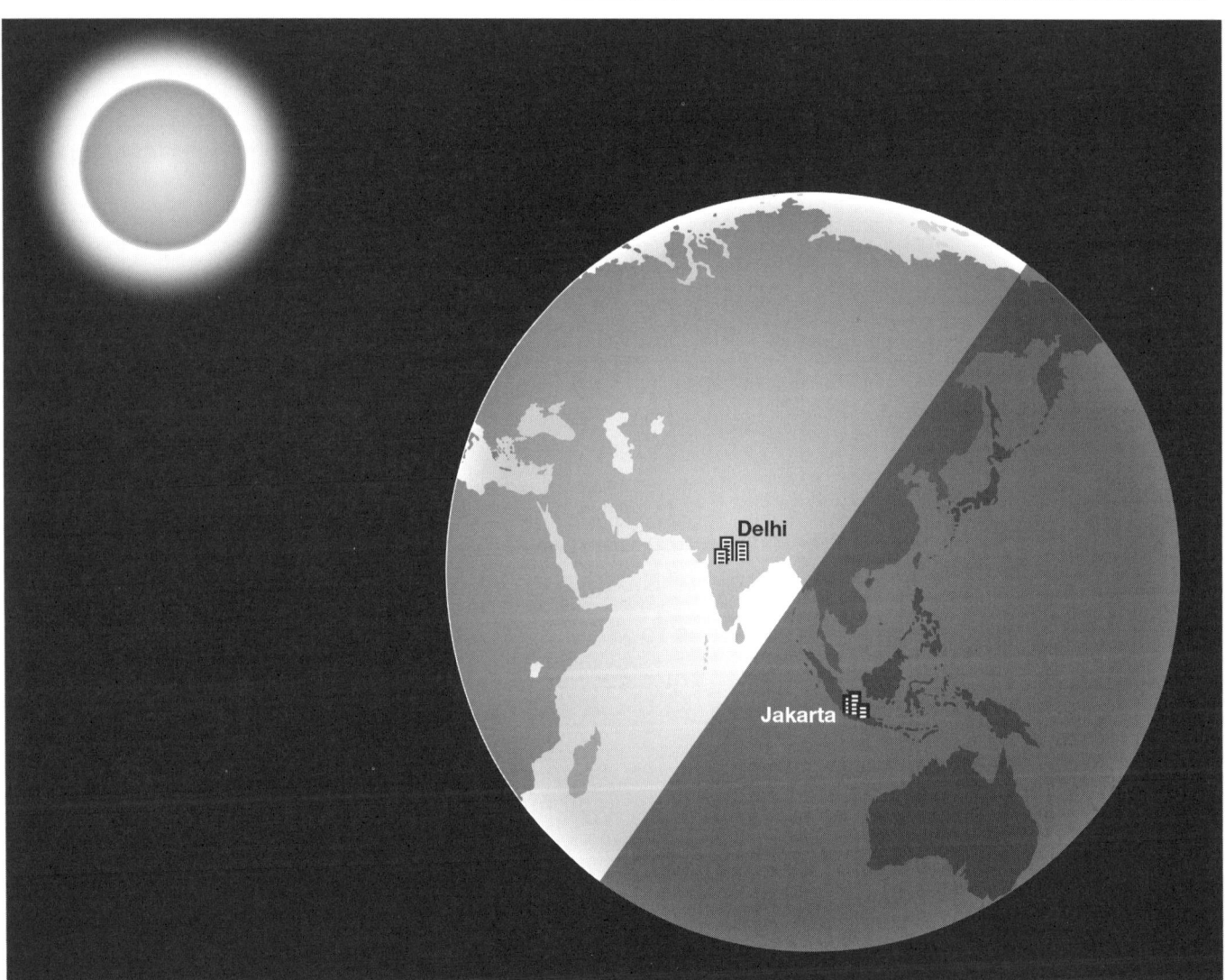

1. Which city is in daylight? _____
2. Which city is in the dark? _____

The Earth is like a spinning ball

The girls have made a model to show day and night.

The ball is planet Earth and the torch is the Sun.

1. Is it day or night at the X? _____

2. What will happen to the X as the girls slowly turn the ball in the direction of the arrow?

   _____

3. **Think about it!**

   If the Earth did not spin, what would happen to day and night if you lived on the dark side?

   _____

CHECK YOUR LEARNING

○ I know that we get day and night because the Earth spins.

6.2 Does the Sun move?

It looks like the Sun is moving

It is morning. The Sun gets higher in the sky.

The boy is on planet Earth, which spins. The Sun is still, but looks as if it is moving.

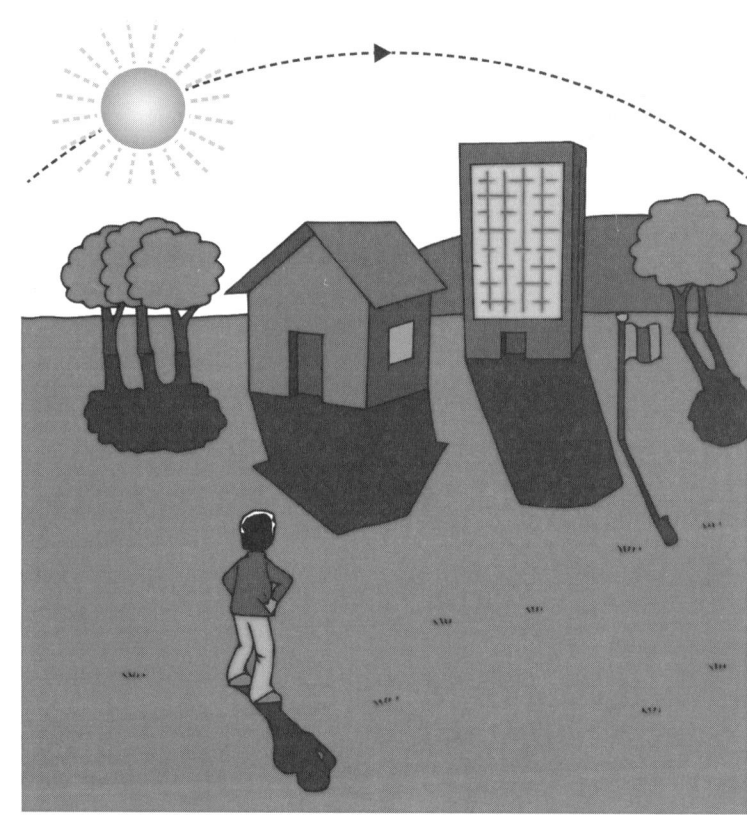

1. At 12 o'clock the Sun will be over the house. Draw a circle to show where the Sun will appear.

2. Late in the afternoon, the Sun will be over the flag. Draw a circle to show where the Sun will appear.

3. Choose the right words to finish this sentence.

   The Sun looks like it moves because

   _____

   _____

   the Earth is still.   the Earth spins.
          the Sun is moving.

   ⚠ Never look straight at the Sun. It can damage your eyes.

Confused Khushi

Khushi is confused.

1 Finish this letter and draw a picture to help Khushi.

I see the Sun go across the sky every day. It must move.

Dear Khushi,

The Sun looks like it moves but _____

_____

_____

_____

_____

2 Think about it!

If the Sun was right above you, would you have a shadow? _____

CHECK YOUR LEARNING

○ I know that the Earth spins and it looks like the Sun is moving.

6 The Earth and the Sun   41

6.3 Changing shadows

`unfair`

Shadow hand

You will need a bucket of soil or sand, and a pole.

LOOK AND LEARN

Shadows are short when the Sun is high in the sky. Shadows are long when the Sun is low in the sky.

The children have made a shadow stick. They have drawn the shadow each hour this morning.

1. Predict and draw in the shadows for

   a 1 o'clock

   b 2 o'clock

   c 3 o'clock.

2. Write the time by each shadow.

3. Make your own shadow stick and repeat this activity outside.

CHECK YOUR LEARNING

○ I know that shadows move slowly as the Earth spins.

○ I know that shadows are short when the Sun is high and long when the Sun is low.

Remember:

Keep your shadow stick in the same place or your test will be **unfair**.

Answers

1 Going outside

1.1

Sorting animals

2 and **3**

4 Think about it!

A fish cannot live in a flower pot because it needs (to live in) water (to breathe).

1.2

A better environment

1

2 Think about it!

Litter is bad for animals because it can hurt them if they eat it or it can cut them if it is sharp.

1.3

What is the weather?

1 and **2**

	Weather	Temperature
	snow	cold
	rain	cold
	wind	warm
	cloudy	warm
	storm	cold
	sunny	hot

2 Looking at rocks

2.1

Sorting rocks

1 to **4** The learner will collect their rocks, sort them based on their appearance and draw them in the table.

Answers 43

2.2
Which rock is hardest?

1 Use the same force for each rock. ✓
Use the same coin for each rock. ✓

2 Answers will depend on the rocks used.

3 *Think about it!*
The best rock to use for making steps will be the rock that is the hardest. So it will have the smallest or no scratch.

4 It is the hardest rock so the steps will not get scratched or wear out.

2.3
What is soil?

2 Answers will depend on what is found in the soil.

3 *Think about it!*
yes ✓   There is air in soil. Animals need air to breathe.

2.4
Where do natural materials come from?

1

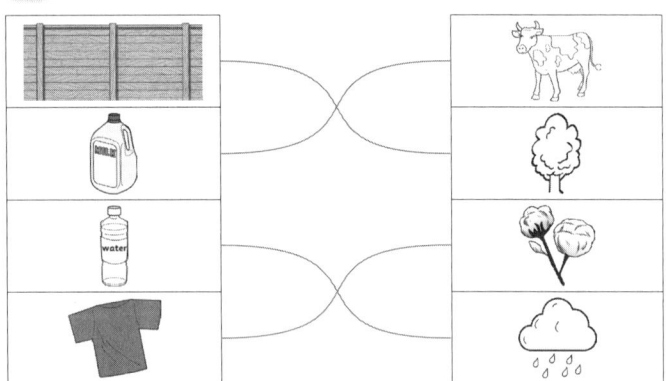

2 *Think about it!*
Any three man-made materials. For example: glass, plastic, card, nylon, polyester, brick, concrete, fizzy drinks, chocolate, fibreglass, carbon fibre. Learners might suggest some metals (iron, steel, brass, tin, aluminium, zinc, lead, bronze and titanium are all man-made materials; gold, silver, platinum and copper can be found naturally).

3 Changing materials
3.2
Materials that bend and twist

1 and **2**

Object	Material	Bend	Twist
sheet of paper	paper	✓	✓
paper clip	metal	✓	✓
T shirt	cotton	✓	✓
coin	metal	✗	✗
ruler	plastic	✓	✓

3 *Think about it!*
It would be hard to bend and twist. (You might walk like a robot!)

3.3
Testing elastic materials

1 Answers depend on learner's predictions.

2 to **4** Sponge and rubber are elastic. Paper is not elastic.
Metal is elastic until it is bent or twisted too far then it is not elastic. If learners have used a small force to bend or twist it, the correct answer is 'elastic'. If they have used a larger force, the correct answer is 'not elastic'.

5 *Think about it!*
Bouncy balls, trampolines, cuddly toy animals and Jack-in-a-boxes all use elastic materials.

3.4
A melting candle

1 and **2**

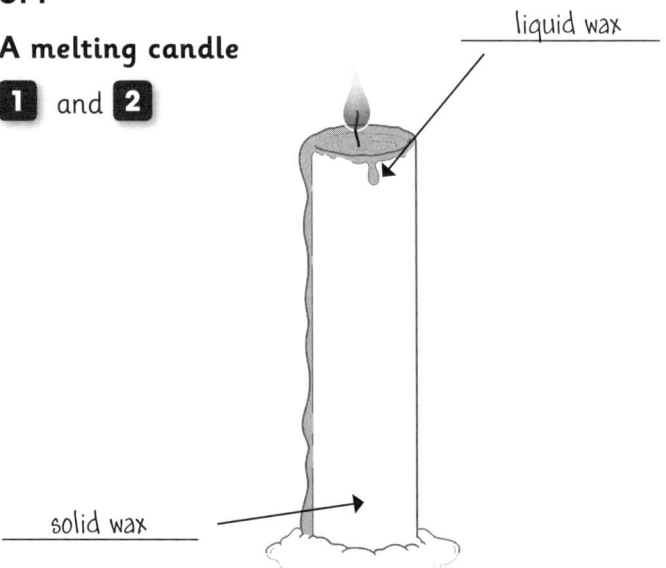

liquid wax

solid wax

Melting ice

3 make it colder ✓

4 Think about it!
The rock has melted (to make lava).

3.5

Dissolved or not

1 Sugar: The sugar has dissolved.
Salt: The salt has dissolved.
Sand: The sand has not dissolved.
Sweets: The sweet has not dissolved. OR The sweet is dissolving slowly.

2 Sweets

4 Light and dark

4.1

Different light sources

4.2

Can I see in the tent?

2 The learner should report if any objects were easier to see. White or shiny objects should be easier to see in the dark.

3 The black objects should be harder to see.

4 After they use the torch, the learner should comment on whether this helped them.

5 Think about it!
The learner might talk about a little light coming under a door, through the curtains or around the side of the curtains. Any reasonable explanation should be accepted.

4.4

Shadow show!

1 1. a girl, 2. a balloon, 3. a bicycle, 4. a plant/flower, 5. a frog, 6. a rabbit, 7. a butterfly, 8. a bird.

Turn it, change it

1 to **4** The learner should have recording drawings in the table of the shadow of each object and then the shadow after turning the object.

5 Electricity

5.1

Does it use electricy?

2 Which of these objects use mains electricity and which use a cell? Tick one box.

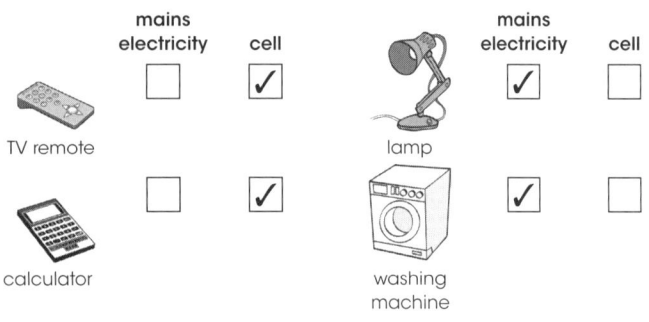

Electricity around me

1 and **2** The learner will have identified different electrical items and said if they use mains electricity or cells.

3 **Think about it!**

The learner will talk about an electrical machine they would miss if they had no electricity.

5.2

Danger, danger!

2 The learner should talk about avoiding the dangers around mains electricity, water and electricity, trailing leads and damaged wires.

5.3

My electric circuit

1 The learner should follow the circuit on the page and be able to point out the cell, wire and bulb.

2 and **3** The learner should make a circuit. If their circuit worked, they should talk about the circuit being fully connected and about electricity moving around the circuit.

46 Answers

5.5

Make a switch with a straw!

1 and **2** The learner should make a prediction followed by a test. The metal clip should make the connection and the circuit should work.

4 The learner should talk about the switch being on or off, connected or not.

6 The Earth and the Sun

6.1

City in the day or night?

1 Delhi

2 Jakarta

The Earth is like a spinning ball

1 day

2 The X will move to the dark side, so to night-time.

3 *Think about it!*
It would be never-ending night.

6.2

It looks like the Sun is movIng

1 The circle will be high above the house – the highest point in the Sun's path.

2 The circle is drawn over the flag but lower in the sky now.

3 The Sun appears to move because the Earth spins.

Confused Khushi

1 A letter is written to Khushi explaining that the Sun does not move, that the Earth is spinning and that this makes the Sun appear to move across the sky. The learner may add a drawing to help explain.

2 *Think about it!*
Yes, you would have a shadow but it would not look like your body – it would just be a very short shadow around your feet.

6.3

Shadow hand

1 Lines should be drawn to the left of the 12 o'clock shadow. 1 o'clock slightly to the left and slightly longer, the others more to the left and a little longer.

2 The times should read 1 o'clock to 3 o'clock from right to left.

3 The learner should carry out the task and record what they find.

Glossary

1 Going outside

cloudy	weather when there are clouds in the sky
cold	a temperature which is low
different	not the same
environment	a place where animals and plants live
hot	a temperature which is high
litter	unwanted materials that people have dropped
rainy	weather when water falls in drops from clouds
snowy	weather when ice falls in soft, white flakes
stormy	weather with strong wind, a lot of clouds and rain, and sometimes thunder and lightning
sunny	bright weather that happens when the Sun is shining
temperature	how hot or cold something is
Venn diagram	a way of sorting things using overlapping circles
warm	a temperature between cold and hot
windy	weather when the air moves around

Remember: Practise saying these words aloud. Try to use them when talking about the topic.

2 Looking at rocks

air	the gas all around us that animals need to breathe
cotton	a soft, white, fluffy, natural material that comes from the cotton plant
died	used to be alive but is not now

fair (test)	a test where you only change one thing and keep the other things the same
force	a push or a pull
hard/er/est	strong and not easily dented
living	alive
man-made	made by people – not found in nature
milk	a natural white liquid that comes from cows and other animals
natural	comes from nature (from the ground or from plants or animals) – not man-made
scratch	a dent or mark in a surface
soil	the natural material on the surface of the Earth in which plants grow
wood	a natural material that comes from trees

3 Changing materials

bend	to change the shape of an object so that it becomes curved or folded
dissolve	when a solid becomes part of a liquid, for example salt dissolves in water
elastic	an elastic material can stretch but then goes back to the shape it started as
heat	to make hotter
ice	water that has become solid
liquid	a material that can flow or be poured – water is a liquid, for example
melt	to change from a solid to a liquid
solid	a material that keeps its shape and does not flow

squash	change the shape of an object by pushing or crushing it – making it shorter
stretch	change the shape of an object by pulling – making it longer or wider
twist	change the shape of an object by holding one end and turning the other

4 Light and dark

dark	when there is very little light or no light
light	bright glow from a light source that allows us to see things
Moon	the large object that goes round the Earth and we see in the sky at night
reflect	if something reflects light, the light shines back from that object
shadow	an area of darkness we see when an object blocks light
Sun	the nearest star to Earth – it gives us light and heat
torch	a small object you hold in your hand which uses a cell (battery) to make light

5 Electricity

battery	a store of electricity, also called a cell
bulb	a glass ball or tube that lights up when electricity passes through it
cell	a store of electricity, also called a battery
circuit	a complete path that electricity can flow around
connected	joined together
electric shock	when electricity goes into your body – a big shock can hurt or kill you
electricity	we use it to make things like lights, computers and televisions work
mains electricity	powerful electricity we use in buildings
power cables	big wires that carry a lot of electricity across a country; they are very dangerous
predict	to say what you think will happen
switch	something that can break the flow of electricity in a circuit
wire	a piece of metal that electricity flows through – we use it to connect things in a circuit
working circuit	a loop that electricity can flow around

> **Remember:** Practise saying these words aloud. Try to use them when talking about the topic.

6 The Earth and the Sun

day the time when a place on Earth is facing the Sun – the hours of daylight

night the time when a place on Earth is facing away from the Sun – the hours of darkness

spin to turn round and round about a point

unfair (test) a test where you change more than one thing